# Grow a Flower

Margaret Clyne

This is my flower.

You can grow a flower, too!
This is how you do it.

# You will need:

seeds

a little pot

4

a big pot

string

soil

a watering can

a stick

little pot

Put the soil in the little pot.

seed

Then put the flower seed
in the soil.

watering can

Next, water the soil.
Put the pot in the sun.

8

The roots and shoots are growing.

leaves

stem

The stem and leaves are growing.

The bud is growing into a flower!

You can grow a flower, too!

12